Letter To My Imagination

212 Short Meditations

To Help You Overcome Rejection,

Discouragement, and Fear of Failure—

And Start Being More Creative

Nicolas Cole

*This book
is dedicated to
the wounded
inner child.*

Nicolas Cole is an author, and the #1 personal development writer on the internet with more than 75,000,000 views on his work.

Cole rose to internet stardom in 2015 when he became the #1 most-read writer on Quora, accumulating tens of millions of views on his viral articles, and his work being republished in TIME, Forbes, Fortune, Business Insider, CNBC, The Chicago Tribune, and more. In 2016, Cole became one of Inc Magazine's Top 10 contributing writers, accumulating millions of views on his business & creativity column, and in 2017 he founded a ghostwriting and thought leadership agency called Digital Press, for Fortune 500 executives, Silicon Valley founders, venture capitalists, Grammy-winning musicians, Olympians, NYT best-selling authors, international public speakers, and more.

Cole has written three books: *Confessions of a Teenage Gamer*, a memoir about his high school years as one of the highest-ranked World of Warcraft players in North America (while undiagnosed with Celiac Disease); *Slow Down, Wake Up: 150 Short Meditations For A More Present Life*; and *Letter To My Imagination*.

He lives in Los Angeles, but will forever be from Chicago. For more information, please visit www.nicolascole.com

Dear Imagination,

I'm sorry.

I've had a tough time hearing you—because I ran away.

The last time we hung out, we got in a lot of trouble. Good trouble, the kind I don't regret, but trouble still and I don't like being punished. It makes me feel wrong, like I'm not good enough and never will be.

I hope you can understand.

I'm writing to say I miss you though. You're my very best friend. And since you've been away—since "I've"—been away—things haven't been the same. Life feels like a rusty set of gears: all oil, no color.

How have things been for you?

I have a few ideas I haven't shared with anyone and I think you might like them. If you want to hang out again, that is. I promise I won't run away this time. (I've grown a lot since our last adventure.)

Anyways, let me know.

Cole

(Imagination writes back…)

"What are you thinking?"

1. What's The Point?

Whenever I've tried to write
in the past two years (SAD!),
I've stopped at the question,
"What's the point?"
I used to know.
The kid in me was in love
with exploring the world in him—
until it was crushed.
Now, the point just seems to be
money. Or progress.
Two things I can measure.
But neither has given me
the lasting joy that comes from imagining.
So I've been chasing more lately,
hoping to stop feeling so without.
And with each step, I believe in my pursuit more—
I have to, to keep it alive.
But with each step,
I also believe less and less
in what I knew my purpose once was.
Stuck,
endlessly in motion,
I'm exhausted
from spinning my wheels.

2. Fast Lane

I said I wanted
the fast lane.
Now that I'm in it,
and cars are whizzing by,
I think often of
the slower way of life.

I'd be lying if I said
I didn't crave it.

3. Curved Spine

A curved spine
is a sign you're not centered.
When you lean too far to one side,
you're leaning away from the other.
Why?
What's over there that pushed you so far?
What are you running from?
A curved spine—
you're not aligned,
and there's a reason.

4. Stealth

Today,
Matt and I drove up into the hills.
We walked to the side of the road
with a clearing.
He pointed to a house
in the far corner and said,
"Look at that—stealth."
Black angles on the flat roofs,
and all I could say was,
"I'll have it."

5. Inspiration

I fear inspiration now.
Ever since I sat on the couch,
the center of my family circle—
my latest expression, *Confessions*,
vibrating on the table.
Evil. Manipulative. Psychotic.
Just a few of the words used
to describe me.
"My inspiration is to blame."
And I took it,
and took it,
until there was nothing left to take—
and nothing left of me.
The rage was gone.
Even the sadness slowed to a still.
On that couch, I sat, numb,
wondering whether I would ever
be inspired again.

That last time brought so much pain,
I fear inspiration now.

6. Follow The Feeling

Trace down your heart,
into your spine,
and around your waist.
Do you breathe?
Or do you
constrain yourself,
afraid of what you'll find:

a part of you
that doesn't get heard
enough.

1. Ojai

Oh…

…

…

…

…

…hi.

8. Open Air

Middle of nowhere
is somewhere special.
The stars tell me I'm small.
Cold wind reminds me I'm alive.
Detached from my normal
day-to-day responsibilities,
I can dream again.

9. You Forgot

You worked so hard
to get to a place
where you could earn what you earned before,
for less time.
When you got there,
you forgot the goal was to have more time—
not more money.
Ever since, you've earned much more than before,
but it has cost you more time.
Now, free time to you
means you aren't making enough.

A vicious cycle,
isn't it?

10. In or Out

Dedicated to David S. Rose

You once told me,
"It all depends.
Do you want to be a narrator
of life? Or a player in it?"
I thought I wanted to be out—
to write about the world as I saw it.
But since being in—
oh, since being in the game—
I'm not sure anymore.
Do I want to be In
or Out?

11. May My?

May my
imagination run wild?
Am I given permission
to shine a flashlight on the
unexplained?
Can I pretend to be someone else—
myself, in another life?
Who says I can't
create my own world
out of this one?

May,
my imagination was born.
5/23/1990

12. Staring

Is this what Picasso meant
when he warped chairs
in blurred rooms
making paintings?

Stare long enough
at the energy around you,
and you'll see it too.

13. Gone, Gone

Gone, gone
has the "me" been
who used to crave silence
instead of noise.
Gone, gone
is the 'me" who had built
a routine around joy—
now I'm too busy.
Gone, gone
is the child in me
who lived to play
in the present moment.
Gone, gone.
I can't find him.
And I've been SAD! ever since.

14. Hard

When things are hard,
make them easy.
Touch their stone.
Feel your fingertips.
Let it break
into love.

15. The Hardest Lesson

The hardest lesson to learn in life
is anything emotional you want but don't have
is because you're not giving it to yourself.
Time.
Acceptance.
Love.
Patience.
Until this truth is learned,
you will seek, blame others for your absence,
fume and erupt and cry over how full
everyone else's cup is compared to yours.
Don't worry.
Soon you will realize
that in your other hand is a pitcher—
and you can pour yourself as much as you'd like.

16. Clenched

My struggle "feeling"
is more of a struggle than I thought.
I'm clenched.
The last time I "felt,"
hurt.
I don't want to go through that
again.
So I protect myself
by being clenched
all the time.

17. Blue Eyes

Sometimes,
I wonder if you can see
the red hurt
in my blue eyes.

18. Within You

The relationship you have
with yourself
is a reflection
of the relationships you have
with everyone else.

19. Inner Child

I yell at yours
because they yelled at mine.
I tell you, in escalating tones,
you're the one at fault—
deep down, I'm upset at myself.
I scold you
because I've been scolded for so long.
You're just a child like me though.
By the fireplace, I tell you the truth:
whenever I hurt you,
it's because I hurt too.

I know that's no excuse.

20. Palm Tree

I love you
from the same deep part of my heart
that loves to write.
When I don't write,
I see that loss reflected in your eyes—
and it kills me.

21. FEEL IT!

You used to say to me,
"Feel it!"
You must have known
 how hard that was for me.

22. How Do I?

How do I
take the next step
deeper
into who I know
I can truly be?

"First," a voice says,
"Ask yourself who you already are.
Then drop the 'I.'"

23. Visiting Chicago

You feel like
a younger version of me.
Trains and cold walks—
this was before the palm trees.
Visiting Chicago
reminds me of what it was like
to grow up.

The nostalgia of childhood
will never get old.

24. Matt's Spare Room

My reason to come home.
A place to crash,
to rest, to reflect.
Pillows on the bed
that hold my head with care—
I don't always feel that there:
LA.
Friendship and familiar places,
memories of manifestations
back when they were just dreams.
This room means something to me.
In a way,
it is my home away from
Home.

25. 1.5

"You can only be really great
  at one thing," said Matt.
"At most, 1.5."
Writing, lifting, music,
entrepreneurship—
oh, and my relationship.
1.5.
1.5.
Choosing is a daily struggle.
I want to be great at them all,
and I still want to work on myself.

"That's the good fight worth fighting for,"
  he said.

26. Ownership

If you're not getting
the things you seek in life,
it's your responsibility
to give them to yourself.

21. Entrepreneur v.s Writer

Start associating yourself
more with the second.

That is,
after all,
who you truly are.

28. Quiet Time

Manifest Your Desires
and then close your eyes.
Let your breath find your center—
You'll know when you've arrived.
Sink until you sway.
Feel how it feels to feel.

This is your quiet time.

29. The Day Moves

The day moves
faster than my pen can capture.
In this life of frames,
I can only paint a handful.
And since it will take years
to master the craft
of re-telling,
I must choose wisely.

30. Fortunate

I'm fortunate
for all the gifts and luxuries
I have in my life today.
Honesty and commitment
are what got me here.
But please don't underestimate
the difference between
outward work ethic
and inner work.

31. What's Next?

Create yourself anew.
Longevity is the ability
to reinvent yourself.

Be a beginner again.

32. On This Monday

Quieter than normal,
on this Monday few arrive
to the coffee shop.
Morning drags the rest.
Seems they're playing catch up
instead of arriving at our normal time.

No Monday morning rush.
Just me and a few others.

33. Startup Founder

I want to be
a different kind of startup founder.
Music instead of multi-tasking.
Meditation instead of micro-management.
Business is just the act.
Heart is what you bring to the table.
And passion is how you play it.

34. The Challenge Of Success

The hard part
of succeeding in this world
goes from the desire of making money,
to knowing you could make more
and deliberately choosing
to do things for your soul instead.

35. First Night

The first night
in a long time
dedicated to Cole:
a lift,
music,
writing.

Remember me?

36. The Adult

Most people love the adult.
The adult is dependable,
always there when you need it.
The adult doesn't ruffle too many feathers,
or show people their weaknesses.
The adult acts
in accordance to the situation.
It follows the rules,
obedient to society.

Your inner child doesn't do any of that.

He drops board games all over the basement floor
because he needs to see all the pieces he has
to work with at once.
She reaches for sewing thread from her mother's drawer
before galloping back downstairs to tie
every object together in a beautiful messy maze.
Your inner child plays,
and the adult sees their own rigidity.
Your inner child sings,
and the adult hears only the absence of their own song.
These reflections disrupt the adult,
make it upset.
And so the adult tells the child to stop.
Grow up.
Until the child believes it entirely,

stops playing,
and walks around just like It.

31. Easy

Being upset is easy.
Anyone can burn themselves up,
crackle and flame.
What's hard is being water.
Let them punch you
right in the heart.
Their fist will break
against your waves,
their arm will move in slow motion,
and you will absorb them
while they sizzle.

38. Need you?

Need you say more
to the ones who don't listen?

The righteous judge says,
"I must show them what they don't know."

The quiet observer says,
"Seeing them forget reminds me I sometimes forget too."

Which are you?

39. My Stress

When I don't empty my "piss bucket,"
my stress pulls me down.
Unhappiness settles in
when I don't make time for
the things that make me happy.
Frustration contracts my breath
when I don't ask myself why
I'm frustrated.

My stress
is in my control.

I think that's the hardest part.

40. Missed Mornings

I could have woken up earlier—
I did wake up earlier.
6:40 a.m… but then I snoozed.
So by the time I arrived to
the coffee shop
to write,
I only had an hour—
when I could have had three.
Imagine all we could have done
with three hours.
It would have been like
a honeymoon night after oysters,
I'll tell you that.

41. Feel The Whir

Whether you want to admit it
or not,
the whir of working
is taxing on you.
And although certain moments might not seem that taxing,
even an idle engine uses gasoline—
and after enough time
will overheat.

42. Shingles

A band tight around my ribs,
this sickness shows me
how badly I need to slow down.
Old letters upon graduation,
a time of fear:
"How will I ever support the
artist in me?"
Today, I have that support.
And yet I reach,
and I reach,
for more "ground" to stand on.

At a certain point,
financial stability
is no longer all that's needed.
What good will solid ground do
for a kid who
wants to fly?

This is my time—
a time I have worked tirelessly
to create for myself.

Is it ghostwriting you want
to fuel your fortune?

You're no ghost, Cole.

43. Thinking About Death

If I was to die
today,
this is how I would have liked
to spend my last moments.
Writing.
for myself—and anyone willing to listen.
That is telling,
and should tell me something
about what fulfillment means
for me.

44. I'm Sorry

I'm sorry for abandoning you
in your darkest hour.
I apologize for running
the other way
when you needed me most.
I regret leaving you behind.

Coping got me nowhere fast.

I'm sorry.
Do you forgive me?

45. Pain

A pounding head
can do wonders
for reminding you
how fortunate you are
to have a beating heart.

46. Rough Week

Most of my time
has been spent
sleeping, or awake and
in pain.
It has been a rough week.
But still,
I am appreciative
for this slow time.

I need more of it.

41. Recovery

Stay slow.
Let the body recover.

The wind will be
at your back again
in no time.

48. D. I?

Do I really need
the cars and the money and the house?
Or do I just need a
quiet place
to explore myself?

(I'll take both.)

49. I Used To

I used to
shut myself away
in my bedroom like this, all day
playing video games.
That was my world—
and my imagination loved it.

50. Atmosphere

Is it a career in music I crave?
Or just a bedroom
doused in music,
dedicated to the expression
that happens
when a boy spends enough hours
by himself
at his desk
creating?

51. MORE

I want more of this.
I need more of this.
I cannot let another year,
another day, another hour go by
without dedicating what I write
to my own vision.
Ghosting was never my ambition.
What pays the bills will never satisfy my vision.
It's time I listen.

Grind,
so that you can spend the rest of the night
exploring that place in you
where all the words fall from.
There is so much more
to discover.

Book 1 was just the beginning.

52. GHOST

Sure,
the money's great.
But can you live with
knowing
no one will ever know
it's You?

53. Pivot

The first leap was the hardest.
The second takes more intention.
At first, you wanted money.
You proved that times ten times ten.
But now, you've come to realize,
"I'm worth way more than I'm making."
10 grand can't buy your dream—
all it can buy is a vacation.
This is your time, so
listen up.
You're the one whose pen they want.
There's a reason why they pay so much.
You've got the thing they want.
And it's not words or even sentences—
it's belief, a voice unrushed.

It's yours.
You shouldn't lend it out so often.

54. Priorities

So many ways to express myself.
So many avenues pull at my GPS.
What is my destination?
Where am I trying to get so fast?
And more importantly,
what is my necessary time of arrival?

Otherwise, I'll detour.

55. My Heart

I make a song,
and my heart opens up.
I feel connected to Source again.
When I wake up the next morning,
I feel reenergized,
calm, open, in tune—
music did this, surely.
What rushes to mind next
are all my responsibilities:
the minutia of day-to-day life.
It's open-heart surgery I crave though.
I long for the lab.
Instead, I sit at my desk
and knock items off my to-do list,
all the while whispering to myself,
"Eh—music is just a hobby anyways."
There is a sadness to this mantra.
And the worst part is
a good part of me believes it.

56. One Step Back

One step back
to take one hundred steps forward.
Say "No" to short-term sprints,
and "Yes" to the epic you're scoring.
If it's not of epic proportions,
don't do it.
It's not worth the effort.
What's another ten grand going to get you?
Ten grand is a month of brilliance missed.
Ten grand is weeks of stress.
Ten grand is too much coffee, not enough rest.
Ten grand is another book without your name on it—
someone else getting the credit.
Ten grand isn't worth living a life that isn't mine.

The struggles of a ghostwriter
stepping into sight.

51. My Future

Bank on Nicolas
and Cole withdraws.

Nobody saved anything
that way.

58. Tunnels

Careful
not to lose sight
of the world around you
chasing tunnels.
What they make up for
in efficiency,
they lose in perspective.
You don't want to live your life in the dark
chasing the light at the end,
do you?

59. Everything

Everything you desire
can be attracted.
It just takes intention,
unwavering commitment,
and time.
Which of these 3
are you depriving yourself of?

60. Energy

If you're going to create something,
bring an energy
worth paying attention to.

61. Spaces

You need space in your heart
to love.
You need space in your mind
to think.
You need space in your body
to feel.
The question isn't,
"How can I DO these things more?"
The question is,
"What am I doing so much
there isn't enough space to begin with?"

62. Candles Dancing

The way candles dance,
Renaissance ballrooms would be put to shame.
All their upside-down wine glasses
spinning away and toward tailcoats.
The real performance is happening on the walls.
Just watch how the wicks stand still,
and one hundred gorgeous flames
dance separately

as one.

63. Cobalt Blue

Sink into meditation.
Wait to feel awareness envelop all that you are.
Smile—
you've let go of your Self.
Now open your eyes.
Witness the world
in cobalt blue.

Imagine if you were here all the time.

64. No 2 Feelings

No 2
feelings are the same.
Shades on a blended palette,
they share similarities
but not concrete colors.
Feelings change when they turn
wet to dry.
Feelings turn coarse to touch
over time.

No 2 feelings are the same.
Let this one be
as it is—
because it won't remain.

65. Who Dare?

Who dare
interrupt
this quiet time
dedicated to myself?

The culprit is often
Me.

66. Promise

If you kept
promises to yourself
half as often
as you gave them to other people,
you wouldn't feel so without.

67. Much

It doesn't take much
to take care of yourself,
and spend more time
doing the things you love.

What's expensive
is taking care of
an Ego
that wants it all.

68. Startup Life

Had I known
entrepreneurship
would mean putting
every other person, thing,
activity, or project
in life
ahead of myself,
I'm not sure I ever
would have done it.

69. Ryan's Cabin

A space
where it's encouraged to imagine,
and yin feels easier than yang.
A place
where the trees look 3D,
the way they run lines up and down the mountains.
A room
where an abundance of tools
shows you the joy in simplicity.
And stars
you don't see downtown LA—
or any downtown, for what it's worth.

Ryan's Cabin,
right in time for my 28th birthday
shows me more than anything:
I made some really great decisions.
Music wasn't for me.
Not professionally.

I love it too much
for it to be my profession.

Separating business and art
was the greatest decision
I ever made.

10. Cellos In The Forest

Inspiration
comes in all forms.
To which sound
does your ear turn?

11. What's Worth Having

What's worth having
is somewhere you can hear
the birds chirp,
and the trees sing,
and see the quiet, original
beauty of the world,
undisturbed.

What's worth having
is being able to hear yourself.

12. Enough Change

Enough of this,
"So much has changed."
You've changed.
And yet, through it all
you've remained the same.

So.
What's next?

13. Hearing Aid

I can hear
myself
so much better when
I don't have twelve other
people all
trying to get my attention at
the same time.

14. Pressure

I've grown from the pressure.
I've flown from the pressure.
I know from the pressure
how to flow under pressure.
Try to float on the pressure.
Build a moat for the pressure.
But I know from the pressure
that the pressure never stops.

15. Stress

Stress makes me grow
at an alarming rate.
Red flags are raised
by how quickly I shed my skin.
But I hate the stress because
it means letting go of younger parts of myself—
without being given the chance to say goodbye.

16. Marasprint

This is a marasprint.
I have so far to go—
but I have to get there now.

11. Have I?

Have I woken up
and forgotten my childhood dream?
Has responsibility
beaten out of me
the gift of imagination?
Trace back the journey
and you will find
your dream died the moment you said,
"Wait, I have to do this instead."

And you wait.
And you wait.
And you're still waiting.

18. How Do I?

How do I
know which road to take?
How do I
feel what might be felt
on the other side?
How do I
understand where I am,
where I've been,
and where I want to go
all at once?
How do I—
and the list goes on.

19. Truth

Truth always
looks distorted when
viewed through the lens
of Doubt.
And Hope
wears glasses,
but they hardly help.

80. I Am Happier

I am happier
when I write what I feel.
I am happier
when I sing what's in my heart.
I am happier
when I give myself the space to be heard.
I am happier
when I remember that my Chief Aim
is to stay true to me.

I know when I am happier.

Happiness, then,
becomes a choice—
not a serendipitous blessing.

81. Chief Aim

My Chief Aim
is to live from my heart, and
make decisions based on who I want to be
long term—
not what I want to achieve in the short term.
I aim to stay true to my core self, my creative self,
before I cater to the wants and desires of others.
I aim to prioritize presence and groundedness first, so
all that I do can unfold from the most true
part of who I am.
And I aim to believe in myself,
and support myself,
in all of my heartfelt creative endeavors
moving forward.

82. I Can

I can
do anything I put my
mind to.
Remove the roof.
Let my imagination
pierce through the clouds.
If I can see it,
I can manifest it.

And I can see a lot.

83. What Is Life About?

Life is about
having the freedom
to wake up in the morning
and do the things you love,
that come from the most genuine part of you,
more often than you work.

That way,
the work you end up doing most often
is on yourself—
not for someone else.

84. My First Mentor

Dedicated to Cachexic

My first mentor
taught me the difference
between external rewards
And inner truth.
"Gear won't make you a better Mage,"
he'd say.
Easy for him in all his epic gear,
I thought.

It wasn't until I had it all too
that I learned
he'd been right all along.

85. PvP Videos

Reminders
there's more to this game
of life than
stacking gold, playing the auction house,
raiding for epic gear and
doing daily quests.

What about your creativity
as a player?

86. The First Step

The first step
of knowing yourself
is leaving yesterday behind.
Look to the moment you're in—
no need to imagine the future.
All will reveal itself shortly.
Watch as the waves open up.
No ocean here, just energy.
Listen to the clinks of glasses
and the murmur of chatter
and the stillness you're able to find
in it all.
The first step
doesn't need to be some
grand gesture.
Where you already are
will do.

81. Feel Your Flow

Do what you must,
so long as it is done
for the space you truly need
to be
all that you can Be.

88. Saturday

Saturdays
are for personal progress,
intimate understanding,
and cups of coffee sipped.
A time to know yourself
outside the day to day.
Take Saturdays to see the world
the way you want to see it.

And work Sundays to make daydreams
come true.

89. To Write

To write
is to have a relationship
with yourself.
How do you see the world?
You can tell me.

90. The Coffee Shop

I remember
being 20 years old
working the 5 a.m. shift
at ArgoTea.
The walk through Chicago's hungover midnight
required a full scarf around my face—
it was that cold.
I was out of breath after the
fifteen blocks.
But I didn't mind things so much
once I had my first cup of coffee.
I'd stand at the register
with my apron on, my little brown hat,
and every once in a while I would
rip a few inches of receipt paper off the roll
and grab a pen:
I had an idea.
I'd write down the title of a book,
a few rap lyrics,
explain the sounds I heard in my head
for a song.
And then I'd stuff the receipt into the front
of my apron.
I didn't make much money
working at that tea and coffee shop.
But I still have a folder in my closet
with all those receipts—
and they didn't cost me a penny.

91. Coffee Shops Pt. II

I wonder
how many coffee shops
my pen has played in?

Like a local musician,
this is where it all started.

92. Priorities

You almost
woke up and immediately dove into work.

Instead, you swam into your heart and touched the day.
How much better do you feel?

93. More and Less

You would have so much more
if you understood the power of less.
For example:
you say you want more time.
But in order to have time,
you need less commitments,
less projects, less people asking things of you.
Having less of those things means,
at least in the short term,
less money, less approval, less
of all the things the Ego attaches to.
But look closely at the power of less.
Less commitments.
Less money.
Yes, but so much more time.

It took me
a while to understand too.

94. Storm

When the weight of the wave
exceeds the flex of the mast,
look for the horizon
at the end of the blackness.

95. Afraid

Moments of fear
are what mold
cowards into generals.
Like clay,
a heated softness
keeps you
from cracking.

96. Feels Like Fear

If it grips your chest
and points out a mistake…
If it has your stomach twisting
and your appetite running dry…
If it lets you lose sleep
and keeps your ease at bay…
If it makes you question
who you truly are!
If it feels like fear,
it's fear.

Don't be rude.
Say hello.

91. Distractions

Distractions are
a great way
of avoiding what matters
most.

98. Simple Equation

When I imagine
and then paint what I see,
I reconnect with Source.

When I don't,
I don't.

99. Confidence

Confidence is
imagining where you want to go,
and believing in yourself enough
to know you'll get there—
even if you aren't sure how yet.

100. Running Nose

Mouth hanging open,
a clothespin between the eyebrows, pinching.
Tongue like cotton.
When I lick: the seal of an envelope.
From the nostrils, dripping,
same as a squeezed kitchen rag.
Swallow and the ears make popcorn.
Head is pulled from under water—
relief.
Then the room turns dizzy,
and I look like I've been slapped silly.

101. Alone Time

When I get too much of you,
I need interaction.
When I don't get enough of you,
I'm distracted.
You're a whole relationship in itself—
this relationship I have with myself.
And I'm constantly
in search of balance.

102. Routine

Will I ever find you again?
Or have I learned forever
the benefits of rigidity
don't outweigh
the freedoms of improvisation.

103. Prague

I remember you.
I'd like to return one day.
You were like a dream.
Swallowed me whole.
You gave me a space
to explore the impossible.
You introduced me to Kafka—
my first idol as a writer.
I know you left an imprint on me.
Time will tell how deep that imprint goes.

104. Leadership

I had a moment
out at dinner
with my co-founder and two of our employees.
I started talking and
they all turned to look at me.
I was in charge.
And that hit me like a ton of bricks
because I never saw myself as the "leader."
Just one of them,
doing my best.

I'm learning that's what leadership
really is.

105. A Quiet Day

Not quite sure
what the day is trying to say.
I should let go—
give her some space.
When I step away
I can see more of her pretty smile.

I hope things stay this way for a while.

106. Lazy Weekend

Lazy weekends
are important.
You need them
to play the long game.
Take some time to yourself—
it's yours for a reason.

101. Perfection

My dreams and aspirations
center around perfection—
an idea I have
for acceptance.
"If only I could get it right,
then they would understand me."
But
I don't think
any amount of perfection will
heal the part of me that's hurting.
Even when I'm working
I insist I'm undeserving.
Even if I'm learning,
I fear I'm not learning fast enough.
I swear, all of my seams
are about to bust.

108. Shoulders

Responsibility
when intertwined with love
feels heavy as loss.

109. Is?

Is this
what I really want?
Is it?
I ask myself this question
so many times a day,
I'm not even sure
what I'm asking for anymore.

110. Happy

You are happy
the moment you allow
happiness to flow through you.

Easier said
than done.

111. Where Are You At?

The first question
you need to ask yourself
when the day starts
piling up,
is, "Where are you at?"

After that,
the rest will make sense.

112. Matt's Bachelor Party Weekend

At the airport.
Flight delayed.
Seeing what's most important:
Being Here Now.
Weekend reminders.
Circle of friends.
Thank you for
bringing me back.

113. Fortunate

An open heart
and humility
will never lead you
astray.

114. Creative Destinations

The dream
is to choose
creative destinations,
make something memorable,
and then choose a new destination.

The truth is,
you can do this anywhere.
"Destination" can be
physical, or
imaginative,
or emotional.

115. Nothing Feels Like You

You feel like
a morning breeze—
not an alarm.
You wake me
with a tender touch—
not a jolt.

Creativity is a woman
who needs a partner.
I regret the days I
sit and watch you dance alone.

116. Legacy

My legacy
is to wield the most
creative pen
in the game.
To do that,
I must spend less time
around players whose aspirations
revolve around writing
tutorials.

117. No Need

No need to
get discouraged.
The first step
is always the hardest.
Once the second foot lands,
you're off and
running.

118. Power

Explore your heart.
You'll find scars that,
if acknowledged,
will melt your fears
and show you
your true power.

119. Routine Part II

Routine
is what shows you
progress
in the softest way.

So much more productive
than aimless grinding,
wouldn't you say?

120. Full Moon Meditation

I am ready to let go
of the anger, the sadness,
the betrayal, and the abandonment
I feel toward my family.
I am ready to be one
with them—
and within myself.
I am ready to forgive,
and see the love between us
so that we can heal
and move forward.
I am ready to open my heart
to them,
and to the deepest part of me.

121. Dad's Birthday

There are so many things
my heart wants to say to you.
But we never speak this way.
Excuse me while I take small steps
to open up.

122. Expansion

Expansion on the way.
Nothing is more exciting
than remembering,
and at the same time exploring,
your potential
as a player.

123. Familiarity

There is a happiness
and a calm
that comes with the first
inhale of a morning cup of coffee
before writing.
Without it, I crumble.
With it, my life feels centered and purposeful.

The writing, that is—
the coffee is just a catalyst.

124. How To Quiet

If you can sit
and feel the vibrations of the
jackhammer on the street outside your window
without getting impatient or upset,
you'll know you're meditating.

If you can't stand the sound,
you're still in your head.

125. My Chi

I've never tolerated
people fucking with my chi.

126. Slowness

It's impossible
to feel the slowness of life
if you're swimming faster
than the current's natural rhythm.
What you'll feel instead
is the weight of the water—
and the pressure will frustrate or even crush you.

127. Poems

Poems all
don't come
rushing out at once.

Sometimes,
you have to wait a while
for the right phrase
to arrive to the party.

128. 4th of July

Cole, pre-girlfriend,
would have woken up today
before everyone else
to grab a warm cup of coffee
and get more done
than most people accomplish
in an entire month.

Cole, post-girlfriend,
has the coffee and the morning,
but the rest of the day reserved
for beaches, tequila, and barbeques.

Hey.
I'm trying to find balance.
Okay?

129. One Day

One day,
I will have the luxury
of waking up to my ideas from yesterday.
One day,
I will see a story through
to the end.
One day,
I will hear the mountains whisper,
and the valleys whistle,
and the waterfalls brush their teeth,
and I will lose myself
in my imagination
as I once did as a kid
again.

One day.

130. Launch Weekend

Amazing what a few days,
just a few,
can do for your inner child.

131. Found

The moment
you stop searching
and start welcoming,
is the moment lost
becomes found.

132. Understood

For the past few months,
maybe longer than I realize,
I've felt exhausted.
The sprint pace
has realized its marathon,
and excitement at the future
has slowly fermented to resentment
of the past.
I question my decisions,
and my prioritizing others ahead of myself.
I'm thankful for the journey,
but skeptical of the consequences.
I wonder what my life would be like,
right now,
if I hadn't helped Drew take the leap.
If we hadn't started Digital Press—
and how all of that would have impacted
my relationship with Alyssa.
And then I question how our relationship
would have unfolded—
would I have stayed in Chicago?
Gone to Arizona?
Ended up in LA all the same?
I wonder these things,
because I am aware of the sacrifices I've made,
and how little of my life now
is what I originally leapt it to be.

133. After

I keep saying,
"After."
After what?
When is enough
ever enough?
A better question would be,
"How, now?"

134. "I"

I am a writer.
That's what I do.
Storyteller by nature—
that's what I give to you.
"I" is just a name.
Call me what you want to.
All that truly matters
is if these words ring true.

135. Can't Know

You can't know
what's around the next bend.
All you can know
is whether you want
to find out for yourself.

136. Sometimes

Sometimes
you need a weekend away
to hear what you love most
in your heart.

137. Hotel Room

How many others
have sat here like me,
staring out the window in the morning?
How many others
have shared this bed?
How many have
seen this hotel room,
been pleasantly surprised,
or been discouraged and let down?
How many lives
does a hotel room live?

138. Time

Time
can both drag
and sway,
lullaby and
ignite.

Time is what
you make it.

139. More Fear

The fear in you
is temporary.
Feel it,
embrace it,
breathe into it,
and move beyond it.

The longer you sit with fear,
it won't be there for long.

140. Love and Trust

Love what you create
today,
and trust that even if you can't see why,
you will one day.

141. If.

If there's one thing
I would like to work on,
it would be carving out
silence for myself.

Silence does for my soul
what not many other things
can.

142. Childhood Mornings

What inspires
the inner child
starts with believing
its safe
to imagine.

143. Soften

Are you the stone edges
of the pool?
Or the blue
swashing back and up and over
into the grass?
To harden is to
strike a pose.
To be soft
is to dance.

144. Ironic

When I need it the most,
I give it to myself the least.
When I crave silence,
I numb myself with noise.
When I want to be heard,
I shut my mouth—and then
shut down.

How ironic.

145. What?

What is my Chief Aim again?
What do I truly want—
and why?
What is all this for?
When did I lose sight of my vision?
How do I know I'm on track?
Will things ever feel the same again?
What am I comparing today to?
When I feel unsatisfied, why?
When I want something else, what is it?
Where will I go once I've gotten to where I'm going?
What will it take for me to
slow down and
wake up?

146. Craig

"We should do
  a mastermind for writers,"
  I said.
"I think the math on that
  is about a million dollars," he said.
  I got excited,
  and he lowered his voice.
"But it wouldn't be a big enough
  leap forward for me," he said.
  And then continued:
"I don't mean financially—
  I mean I do, but what I really mean
  is personally."

And I agreed.

Even a million dollars
couldn't fix the wound
inside of me.

147. Nicolas / Cole

Teaching
is only a worthwhile pursuit
so long as you continue to
play yourself.
Otherwise,
how on earth
could you truly teach
a child how to play?

148. Conflict

The key to conflict
is to ask yourself first
where the lock comes from—
why do you feel what you feel?
Instead of immediately reacting
out of anger,
contemplate the lock
before trying to break it open.

149. Cave Creek

Mountains bring out
the best in me.
And when they do,
I see the best in you.

150. Caged

A caged animal
has a sad look in their eye,
living as their told.
That is how you live
when your ego parents your inner child
with no compassion
for the need to run wild.

151. Trail

How could I
have ever
wandered so far from
the trail,
and onto a highway that
I'd forgotten the trees
altogether?

152. She

She loves you
when she takes your shirts,
and wears them as her own.
She wants
another part of you
to hold close.

153. LA

LA,
you've been so good to me.
I leapt,
and fell right into your arms.
You sway in a way
that's soothing.
Your tide washes me out—
I can see Me again.
You appeal to so many different
emotions.
I don't give you nearly
as much credit as you deserve.

154. Tone

Tone is a frequency.
It's the way words sound
standing on the emotion below them.
You cannot write the tone
of an emotion you aren't currently feeling.
And you cannot deliberately shape tone
until you understand the way
tones sound within you.

155. Brilliance

Brilliance
is not a destination.
It's a form of
self-inquiry
that ends with an attempt,
opposed to a resignation.

156. The View

The view
can tell you a lot
about yourself—
and the way you're seeing the world.
Look at
Beverly Hills:
Do you see the palm trees
and rich greenery?
Or the sprawling homes
and expensive cars?

Asked another way:
are you looking through the lens
of achievement
or presence?

151. New Path

This new path
teaches a level of mastery I've ever known.

Self-understanding in silence is
not the same as self-understanding
while leading.

158. Chief Aim V2

Legacy.
Books. Businesses. Expression. Education.
My Chief Aim is to unflinchingly extend
my soul, my perspectives, my talents and
my voice out into the world
for the benefit of all.
I will create and further scale
a life that allows my ideas to manifest in the real world,
while preserving my most valuable asset: time.
I will build empires that
allow me to become exponentially more successful
while allowing for more and more time to
myself and the things I love most.
I will learn to balance both sides of me,
practicing in my daily habits the
control, understanding, compassion, and flow required
to be purposeful as a leader
and forever a student of life.
I will see the trees
before the homes.
I will work to master
myself, first.
"Happy self,
happy everyone else."

159. Stress II

Sometimes,
I get so stressed,
I forget how to connect with Her—
and I feel lost as ever.

160. Help

As I trend downward
on my emotional rollercoaster,
help me hold on and remember
the fall doesn't last forever.

161. Image

Image
is not the same as
imagination.
One provokes the other
and do not forget which.

162. When Was?

When was
the last time
you laid on the couch
with your journal
and asked yourself,
"So what's this all about?"

The fact you can't remember
is the problem.

163. Lost Sight

If you let
too much time go by
without reflecting,
you will lose sight
of why you set down the path you did
in the first place.

164. Like Wind

Needless to say,
who I am today
is already a way's away.
Try to hold wind in your hand—
you can't.
Life is but a sway.

165. Being Good

Being good at
your job
and being good
in life
are two different pursuits.
Don't get them confused.
One does not guarantee the other.

166. Mountains

Mountains
have nowhere to be.
When you're by them,
they reveal your restlessness.
Be like the mountain.
Its beauty comes from
standing still
now and always.

167. Build Order

Where you go in life
is the result of the choices
you make.
Your build order becomes
the compounding effect.

168. Consistency

Consistency is
the act of
doing what you said
you were going to do even
when you don't want
to do it.

169. Questions

Every so often
I catch myself
asking questions,
and so seriously
obsessing over the answer.
I forget altogether
who is aware of the asking
in the first place.

170. Allure

Everything in life
has its allure
right up until the moment
you know you can have it.
Then it slowly fades
as your fingers move closer.
And when you finally grab it,
the allure is gone—
and your eye moves to deeper
or different
desires.

171. Angry Manic Founder

Every morning is a fucking dice roll.
Wake up, not even out of bed yet and I
scroll through my email.
I know I shouldn't, but I do.
I should get my day started on the right foot first,
but I don't.
Instead, a few emails catch my eye:
"Hey, we need to stop using your service," says
one of our biggest clients.
Great.
Wonderful.
As soon as we hit net positive,
we're back in the hole again.
Two days before this, I had a really great investor call—
he wants to put in $100,000.
We still haven't made up our mind on how much we're going to
    raise.
Or if we should raise at all.
Whatever. Amazing.
But before I could even breathe in two full moments of
    excitement,
Drew let me know there's been a conflict
between two employees.
So we have to handle that.
And it just goes on
and on.
This journey will age you quick.

Be careful, and remember the journey needs to be the real
  reward.
Otherwise you'll turn into an
angry manic founder
like me.

172. This Game

Sometimes I
get so caught up in
this game,
I forget why I even started playing
in the first place.

Because it sure doesn't feel like
"play" anymore.

173. E.

Entrepreneurship feels like
trying to make one breath
stretch across a thousand days.

174. When You Notice

When you notice
a slow-falling elevator
on the side of a building under construction,
you're reminded of the descent that comes
with sinking back into who you are.

It doesn't take much.
Just a close look.
One deep breath—and you're right back.

175. Small Moments

Pockets in the day,
small moments,
help you step out of the weeds
to see the forest again.

176. Dayz

Dayz when
I get to write and be creative,
are days when I'm in a daze
in the best way.

111. Holidays

Thanksgiving and Christmas
are coming soon!!!
Nostalgia always warms me in ways
I can't find elsewhere.
A break from getting older?
A love for being young again?
Either way,
somehow
I end up back in my imagination.

178. Listen

When I find myself
writing less,
I should know it's time
to listen more.
There's something underneath my
drive—
a faulty part that must be fixed.

179. Close My Eyes

It's not until I
close my eyes
that I see
how conflicted I've become.

180. Poems

This used to be
a daily practice.
Now I wonder
if they're worth writing
at all.

What's happened to me?

181. Striving

Always striving
for more money, faster—
what is the real goal, Cole?
Instead of a larger paycheck,
and nicer belongings,
here's a question:

What do you want to stand for?

182. Somber

Maybe my writing voice
is somber
because that's what my heart sounds like.

183. Will These?

Will these journals
mean much of anything
in the grand scheme of things
in the end?

184. Misdirected

This is a letter to myself.
I'll try to keep it short.
Ever since I set out to make more and more,
I've fallen overboard.
Like a ship lost at sea, I don't know.

185. I've Stopped

I've stopped
 asking Cole how he's doing—
"What was my dream again?"
And when I stop,
I lose connection.

Disconnected,
I'm without heart.

186. In The Bush

(1st Day in South Africa)

While driving in the jeep
in the bush
in South Africa,
I notice the wonders of the world.
Black rhinos.
Giraffes. And dozens of Zebras.
Water buffalo. A brown hyena.
And multi-colored birds soaring through the sky.
From the moment we landed,
I could feel the "busy" me
adjusting to the pace of the grasslands.
But once the sun set,
and orange filled the sky,
I left it all behind.

Trips like these
always make me think,
"How much happier would I be
living the simple life?"

187. Caravan

Riding as one.
Seeing the world no longer as separate—
what a gift.
I wish more moments in life
felt like this.

188. Inspired?

Inspiration
doesn't just appear
like a sunrise.
It must be found
like a miner in search of coal
who hasn't seen the sun
for seven years.

189. Clarity

I can't know
what's past the glass,
can't see the road in front of me,
can't have clarity
without wiping away the
dirt: obligations.
See more by doing less.

Get out of the way of yourself.

190. Play Out

We'll see
how things play out
balancing conflicting aspirations:
knowing myself more deeply
and conquering the world.
Is it wrong,
or should I say "impossible,"
to share both
at the same time?

191. Artist Cole

I wonder when
I'll take the risks
I know my heart craves so.
So, what will it take?

So, so,
stuck in indifference.

192. Have To

What compulsion
work can thrust upon you,
as a distraction
from the unproductive annoyances of
feeling your soul.
How much easier
to focus on all
the things you have to do—
opposed to surrendering to what could be
in this moment.

Will this inner turmoil
ever stop?
Or does the beauty of life hang
in the tension between what
you love, and what you
have to do?

193. Easy To Forget

It's so easy to forget
the song of the soul.
Careful:
otherwise you'll forget how to
dance too.

194. Begging For Cigarettes

Have you ever noticed
we shut down and reject the
homeless who beg for money,
but reach into our purses and pockets
when they ask for a cigarette?
Maybe it's because we smoke
to ease some sort of pain in ourselves,
and when they ask for relief,
we can relate.
With money, it's harder.
They're asking for the comfort
we struggle most to part with:
Stability.

195. Love Is An Art

Art is like love,
and love is like art.
You cannot force its creativity.
The goal is not to be "productive"
and love as much as you can,
as quickly as you can.
No, to love is to let go of all the things you must do,
should do, have to do,
and lie in bed watching the sun rise
with a naked shoulder pressed gently
onto your collar bone.
And that is how art should be handled.
A morning spent writing
is a morning to make pancakes naked.
Why rush?
The joy is in letting yourself dangle—
not to eat and get dressed.

196. I Wonder

I wonder
where all this will lead?
Suppose wonder
is what calls us to walk forward
in the first place.

197. Only 28

Don't get too lost
in the whirlwind of it all.
You're only 28.
There's so much still to go,
more to explore,
mornings to embrace and long nights.
It's alright.
Just enjoy the journey.

198. Too Much

Too much time away
from the pen here,
and muscles feel as thoughts do
sopped in tequila.

199. Transition

Life for me
used to be a simpler game.
Not quite sure of the point of
stating the obvious.
All great things hide behind great challenges.
Complicated is just another way to describe
beautifully organized chaos.
No sense in missing a simpler past.
Remember when you were there,
and you salivated at the thought of being here?

200. Routine

I'll write this poem
until it happens and
even when it does I'll
still write it to remember:
routine is everything.
You need time to yourself
to create for no one but yourself.
Life without a cadence
has no rhythm—
and a life without rhythm
is a mess.

201. IDEAS

There are so many ideas
on my plate.
So much to get done.
So many steps to take.
Remember, Cole.
This is your time of year
to take a step back.
Give yourself that.
It'll mean more in the end.
Reflect on what went well,
and what went wrong.
Give yourself time to soak—
maybe write a song.
Don't rush, just breathe.
Give yourself what you need.
And don't forget about me…
Don't forget about me…

202. Deep In My Heart

I was writing
my Christmas card to Alyssa
when I felt a door open
deep in my heart.
All of a sudden,
I didn't want to write anymore—
well, I did but
it scared me, and I
was aware of that.
Once I realized what was going on I
pushed myself to walk through
the door and keep writing
from the place love pours
and wounds heal
and the past flickers
and presence sits.
I used to write here,
right here, all the time.
Now, opening the door to this room
in my soul feels like
going into the attic
of a house I've grown tired of living in.
And it makes me so SAD!
This used to be my favorite room
of all.

203. Just

Imagine
how many days go by
that don't get captured
into a poem.

A shame, really.

204. Write The Best

Sometimes I
write the best
when I'm tired.
The harder it is for
me to keep my eyes open the
faster I write and
more easily it flows and
usually the better it is.

205. WATER

When you are water
and the other person is water,
you flow together.
When you fall out of flow,
you fight.
You become fire and the other person becomes fire.
Because at least fire can dance with fire—
and that's as close to flow as you can get.

206. Release

In order to release pain,
you have to find pain and then
push on it.
Break it up.
Help it move.
Avoiding it does no good.
Just dig in,
wince,
and let it be over.

201. Searching For Words

I go crawling on my hands and knees
inside the wet caves of my heart
dripping with
muddy crystal water
searching for words
for you.

208. COATG

A commitment
to self.
A project
with infinite purpose.
Expression
with your name all over it.
Love
to appreciate forever.
COATG,
over and over again,
and you'll live your best life.

209. Fifteen Minutes

Fifteen distracted
unfocused minutes
fly by without you even realizing
where they've gone.

Fifteen quiet,
intentional minutes
feel as long as a lifetime.
And through it all,
you know your purpose:
to be Here
and nowhere else.

210. Chief Aim V3

My Chief Aim
is to live my mission and purpose,
which is to create,
and learn about myself in the process.
I will discipline myself to remove distractions
keeping me from living my life's purpose.
I will be
careful and deliberate with my time
and how I invest it.
I will protect my focus to remain in my most creative, present
    state
for as long as possible at a given time.
I will feed myself
healthy inputs only,
and allow "candy content" in small, infrequent doses.
I will continually remind myself
that to be in love with the process is more important
than achieving the destination.
I will, no matter how tired I am,
play and work on THE EPIC
a little bit each day.
I will sacrifice as many short-term rewards
as I can for the long-term payoffs of
knowledge, expertise, and value.
I will meditate for clarity,
personal growth, emotional understanding,
patience and presence.

And I will embody my mission,
to allow other people to feel the feeling
of living life true to themselves,
by living and creating from that place in me.

I will read this Chief Aim aloud,
every morning and
every night.

211. Where This Comes From

I picked up this practice
of writing short poems in my journal
when I was 19,
after my family rejected
my music—a mixtape titled
Writer's Block.
Suddenly, I was the one
who had writer's block.
And the only thing I could
get myself to write
were these poems.

212. Where's Cole?

We all have a bit of coal in us.

I'll scrape the dirt off
me,
so hopefully you can see
yourself in the reflection.

Author Information

Nicolas Cole Website
http://www.nicolascole.com

Amazon Author
https://www.amazon.com/Nicolas-Cole/e/
B019KMF5B2%3Fref=dbs_a_mng_rwt_scns_share

Goodreads
https://www.goodreads.com/author/
show/14258941.Nicolas_Cole

Smashwords
https://www.smashwords.com/profile/view/nicolascole77

Bookbub
https://www.bookbub.com/profile/nicolas-cole

Quora
https://www.quora.com/profile/Nicolas-Cole-1

Medium
https://medium.com/@nicolascole77

Instagram
https://www.instagram.com/nicolascole77/?hl=en

Twitter
https://twitter.com/nicolascole77

Made in United States
North Haven, CT
23 May 2023

36878495R00133